孔子学院总部 /
国家汉办汉语国际推广成都基地规划教材

走进天府系列教材【成都印象】

游成都

Traveling in Chengdu

西 南 财 经 大 学
汉语国际推广成都基地   著

西南财经大学出版社
中国·成都

西南财经大学
汉语国际推广成都基地 著

总策划 涂文涛

策 划

李永强

主 编

梁 婷 白巧燕

编 者

《成都印象·游成都》 胡倩琳

《成都印象·居成都》 郑 莹

《成都印象·吃川菜》 谢 娟 王 新

《成都印象·品川茶》 肖 静

《成都印象·饮川酒》 谢 娟

《成都印象·看川剧》 郑 莹

《成都印象·绣蜀绣》 谢 娟

《成都印象·梦三国之蜀国》 蒋林益 胡佩迦

《成都印象·悟道教》 沙 莎 吕 彦 陈 茉

《成都印象·练武术》 邓 帆 刘 亚

审 订 冯卫东

英文翻译

Alexander Demmelhuber

Introduction

Traveling in Chengdu is one part of the "Impressions of Chengdu" textbook series, which is promoted by the Chengdu Base of Confucius Institute Headquarters and published by the Southwestern University of Finance and Economics. This book contains 7 units, which are designed on the basis of the Confucius Institute Headquarters'/ Hanban's "International Curriculum for Chinese Language Education" (hereinafter referred to as "Curriculum"), as can be seen, for example, on vocabulary and language points used, and ensures that this textbook is held to scientific, systematic and rigorous standards. The "HSK 4 Exam Curriculum" serves as the standard for the vocabulary and grammar points of this book. It summarizes the famous historical attractions around and in Chengdu, museums, modern leisure life in Chengdu, Chengdu delicacies as well as Chengdu's new tourist attractions. Through studying the Chinese language as a basis, international students are introduced to Chengdu's history and culture. This textbook also aims to provide beginner students with extensive reading material to help them build a strong foundation in Chinese and improve their language proficiency as well as deepen cultural understanding.

Hopefully, you will enjoy *Traveling in Chengdu* and we are looking forward to any criticism or suggestions you might have. Hanban gave us much help and support during editing of this book and we would like to take this opportunity to express our gratitude.

前 言

　　《游成都》是西南财经大学汉语国际推广成都基地推出的"成都印象"系列教材之一。全书共7课，以孔子学院总部/国家汉办的《国际汉语教学通用课程大纲》（以下简称"大纲"）为基本编写依据，涉及《国际汉语教学通用课程大纲》中的大量词汇、语言点等指标，以保证教材的科学性、系统性和严谨性。本书以《HSK4级考试大纲》为词汇与语法的标准，总体概述了成都及成都周边的著名历史景点、博物馆、成都现代人休闲生活、成都美食和成都的新型产业景点等内容，在学习语言表达的基础上向国际学生介绍成都的历史与人文文化，并尝试为初级水平汉语学生增加文化读物，从阅读训练的角度夯实他们的汉语基础，提升其汉语水平及文化理解能力。

　　希望您能喜欢《游成都》这本教材，也希望您对本书提出批评和建议。本书的编写得到了国家汉办的大力支持和帮助，在此一并表示感谢。

目录

第一课 【成都】
Lesson 1 【Chengdu】

① 离开　　líkāi
② 蓉　　　róng
③ 省会　　shěnghuì
④ 地区　　dìqū
⑤ 科技　　kējì
⑥ 商贸　　shāngmào
⑦ 金融　　jīnróng
⑧ 中心　　zhōngxīn
⑨ 交通　　jiāotōng
⑩ 古老　　gǔlǎo
⑪ 历史文化名城
　　lìshǐ wénhuà míngchéng
⑫ 组织　　zǔzhī
⑬ 评　　　píng
⑭ 佳　　　jiā
⑮ 游客　　yóukè
⑯ 锦里　　Jǐnlǐ
⑰ 宽窄巷子
　　Kuān Zhǎi Xiàngzi
⑱ 街　　　jiē
⑲ 历史　　lìshǐ
⑳ 自然　　zìrán
㉑ 休闲　　xiūxián
㉒ 品　　　pǐn
㉓ 春熙路　Chūnxī Lù
㉔ 太古里　Tàigǔlǐ
㉕ 环球中心
　　huánqiú zhōngxīn
㉖ 基地　　jīdì
㉗ 美味　　měiwèi

成都——"一座来了就不想离开的城市"。

成都，又叫"蓉城"，是四川省的省会城市，是中国西南地区的科技、商贸、金融中心和交通中心，是著名的古"南丝绸之路"的起点，也是"一带一路"倡议的重要城市。从古代到现代，成都都有着非常重要的地位。

成都有 4500 多年的历史，是一座古老而美丽的城市。它是中国历史文化名城，也被世界旅游组织评为中国最佳旅游城市，每年来成都旅行的游客超过 2 亿人。现在，走进武侯祠、锦里、杜甫草堂、宽窄巷子，就像打开了一本厚厚的历史书，那些古老的房子、长街都记下了成都的故事。成都不仅是历史名城，而且自然风景也十分美丽。成都附近的山和水，像画一样美丽。

成都，是一座休闲的城市。来到成都，你只需找一个公园，品一杯四川茶，在老茶馆里坐一个下午，跟朋友聊聊天，玩玩游戏；或者约几个朋友，一起到春熙路、太古里、环球中心去，喝喝咖啡、逛逛街、唱唱歌、看看电影，像成都人一样，体会一下生活的慢节奏；你还可以到成都熊猫基地去散散步，了解大熊猫和它们的慢生活。

成都，是一座"美味"的城市。除了传统川菜以外，现在的成都还有许多外地菜，既适合成都人的口味，也适合外地人、外国人的口味。

成都，还是一座现代化的城市，开放时尚。它欢迎来自中国各地和世界各国的人们，越来越多的中外公司也来到了成都，越来越多的人选择在成都工作、生活。

　　成都的美还有很多……看，江一华和文小西也跟着熊猫大萌到成都旅游了，来感受这座"来了就不想离开的城市"。

㉘传统　chuántǒng
㉙开放　kāifàng
㉚时尚　shíshàng

Chengdu is "a city you do not want to leave once you have arrived".

Chengdu, also known as "The City of Hibiscus", is the capital city of Sichuan Province. It is the center of science and technology, commerce and trade, finance as well as transportation in Southwest China. Chengdu is the starting point of the famous ancient "Southern Silk Road" and also an important city of the "Belt and Road Initiative". From antiquity until modernity, Chengdu has always held an important position.

With more than 4,500 years of history, Chengdu is an ancient and beautiful city. It is a famous historical and cultural city of China. It was rated as the best tourist city in China by the World Tourism Organization and over 200 million tourists travel to Chengdu every year. Entering Wuhou Temple, Jinli, Du Fu Thatched Cottage, Kuanzhai Alley nowadays is like opening a thick history book: those old houses and long streets have recorded Chengdu's stories. Chengdu is not only a historic city, but also boasts stunning natural sceneries. The mountains and water bodies near Chengdu are as gorgeous as a painting.

Chengdu is a city of leisure. When you come to Chengdu, you can simply find a park and have a cup of tea in the old teahouse, chatting with friends or playing games, passing a leisure afternoon; or meet up with some friends and go to Chunxi Road, Taikoo Li, the Global Center to have some coffee, go window-shopping, sing and watch movies – just like the people in Chengdu: live slowly. You can also go to the Chengdu Panda Base for a walk to learn about giant pandas and their slow lives.

Chengdu is a city of deliciousness. Apart from traditional Sichuan cuisine, you may also find a wide range of food from other parts of China in Chengdu, pleasing the palates of the locals, non-locals and foreigners alike.

Chengdu, a city of modernity, liberal and stylish. It welcomes people from all over China and other countries in the world. Increasingly more Chinese and international companies are coming to Chengdu and increasingly more people are choosing to work and live in Chengdu.

There is so much beauty to Chendu… Look, Jiang Yihua and Wen Xiaoxi have followed the Panda Da Meng to Chengdu for travel, to experience this "city you do not want to leave once you have arrived".

词语

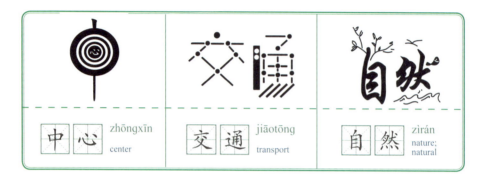

| 中心 zhōngxīn center | 交通 jiāotōng transport | 自然 zìrán nature; natural |

lí kāi 离 开	leave
shěng huì 省 会	provincial capital
shāng mào 商 贸	business and trade
gǔ lǎo 古 老	old; ancient
píng 评	rate

róng 蓉	hibiscus
kē jì 科 技	science and technology
jīn róng 金 融	finance
zǔ zhī 组 织	organization
jiā 佳	good; excellent

chuán tǒng 传 统	traditional
shí shàng 时 尚	stylish; fashion

kāi fàng 开 放	liberal; open; open-minded

专 有 名 词

1. 武侯祠　/ Wǔ hóu cí / Wuhou Temple

2. 锦里　/Jǐn lǐ / Jinli

3. 宽窄巷子　/ Kuān Zhǎi Xiàngzi / Kuanzhai Alley

4. 春熙路　/ Chūnxī Lù / Chunxi Road

5. 太古里　/ Tài Gǔ lǐ / Taikoo Li

6. 环球中心　/ Huánqiú Zhōngxīn / Global Center

语言点

1. 不仅……而且……   2. 除了
3. 既……也……   4. 动词的重叠形式

思考

1. 成都给你的第一印象怎么样？

2. 如果你第一次来成都，你最想了解成都哪些方面的信息？

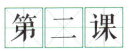

【成都的市内景点】

Lesson 1 【Attractions in Chengdu City】

江一华：

大萌，今天是我和小西到成都的第一天，你带我们去哪儿玩儿？

大 萌：

成都市内有名的景点有天府广场—春熙路、杜甫草堂、宽窄巷子、武侯祠—锦里等，还有很多公园。你们想去哪里？

文小西：

去个人少的地方吧，最好还可以吃好吃的。

大 萌：

我们今天先去杜甫草堂，然后去武侯祠和锦里。明天去天府广场、春熙路和宽窄巷子。

【一】杜甫草堂

江一华：

杜甫草堂真漂亮，这些树又高又大，这些花儿也很漂亮，还有这条小河，河水真干净。

大萌：

你们看，前面那个茅屋就是杜甫的家。

文小西：

大萌，杜甫不是著名的诗人吗？为什么他的房子那么旧、那么小，看起来不太好呢？

大萌：

这是个好问题。那时候，杜甫很穷，工作也不太顺利，他没有钱，连这个茅屋也是朋友们帮他修的。我们现在看到的这个房子是后来重修的。

江一华：

那是怎么重修这个房子的呢？怎么知道它原来的样子？

大萌：

杜甫在成都写了很多诗，从他的诗里我们可以想象他的茅屋的样子，然后再修建起来。

① 干 净　　gānjìng
② 茅 屋　　máowū
③ 著 名　　zhùmíng
④ 诗 人　　shīrén
⑤ 顺 利　　shùnlì
⑥ 连　　　lián
⑦ 后 来　　hòulái
⑧ 重 新　　chóngxīn
⑨ 想 象　　xiǎngxiàng
⑩ 差不多　　chàbùduō
⑪ 一 共　　yígòng

文小西：

杜甫在草堂住了多长时间？写了多少首诗呢？

大萌：

杜甫在草堂住了差不多四年，一共写了二百四十多首诗。他在草堂的时候，自己种地养花。他有一首诗，写的是成都的春雨，非常美。诗的其中一句意思是：春夜下雨，第二天早上看沾着雨水的花，锦官城就像花的世界一样，美丽极了。

【二】武侯祠

① 景 点　jǐngdiǎn
② 参 观　cānguān
③ 套 票　tàopiào
④ 导 游　dǎoyóu
⑤ 免 费　miǎnfèi
⑥ 介 绍　jièshào
⑦ 拜 神　bàishén

大萌：

成都旅游景点参观套票真是又便宜又方便。我们从杜甫草堂到武侯祠，只用了半个小时，车坐起来特别舒服，还有导游免费介绍。

江一华：

嗯，我们去别的景点也坐这个车吧！

文小西：

"武侯"是诸葛亮，那"祠"是什么意思呢？

大萌：

你们最近在学习汉字对吧？那这个"礻"是什么意思？

江一华：

老师讲了，还给我们画了一下，看起来好像一个人在拜神或者死去的人，对吧？

大萌：

对，所以这个"祠"的意思就是纪念死去的人的地方。

文小西：

哦……我懂了，"武侯祠"就是纪念诸葛亮的地方。

大萌：

"武侯祠"不只是纪念诸葛亮，也是纪念刘备的地方。走吧，我们一边参观，我一边给你们介绍吧。

⑧ 纪　念　jìniàn
⑨ 羽　毛　yǔmáo
⑩ 扇　子　shànzi
⑪ 遗　产　yíchǎn
⑫ 区　　qū
⑬ 汉昭烈庙
　　Hàn Zhāoliè Miào
⑭ 惠　陵　Huìlíng
⑮ 三义庙　Sānyì Miào
⑯ 体　验　tǐyàn
⑰ 民　俗　mínsú
⑱ 蜀　国　Shǔguó

江一华：
　这个拿着羽毛扇子的人就是诸葛亮吧？

大萌：
　对。再往前面走是"惠陵"，那是纪念刘备的地方。

　　武侯祠在成都的南边，有三个大的部分：第一个部分是文化遗产保护区，主要包括汉昭烈庙、武侯祠、惠陵、三义庙；第二部分是文化体验区；第三部分是锦里民俗区。在这里，人们可以了解到"三国"之一的蜀国的一些历史，可以看到一些中国古代的书法艺术，还可以看到许多成都传统的工艺品，吃到很多成都的小吃。

【三】锦里

① 旁　边　pángbiān
② 小　摊　xiǎotān
③ 纪念品　jìniànpǐn
④ 味　道　wèidào
⑤ 香　　xiāng
⑥ 特　色　tèsè
⑦ 主　题　zhǔtí
⑧ 值　得　zhídé

大萌：
　逛完武侯祠，我们再看看旁边的锦里古街。锦里虽然是新修的，但可以看到三国时的文化和成都的传统文化。

江一华：
　你们看，那边的小摊在卖纪念品，我要去买一些送给我的家人和朋友。

文小西：
　啊，什么味道？好香！

大 萌：

前面是一条小吃街，卖的全是成都的小吃。

文小西：

锦里真棒，不仅可以买到很多成都传统的纪念品，还有那么多好吃的成都小吃。

大 萌：

是的。成都虽然有好几条古文化街，但是每条文化街都有自己的历史和特点。比如，锦里是以三国文化为主题的古街，宽窄巷子是以清代文化为主题的古街，都很有特色，值得看一看。

【四】宽窄巷子

宽窄巷子由宽巷子、窄巷子和井巷子三条巷子组成，是清代留下来的古街道。现在的宽窄巷子成了商业街，每天都有无数的游客来这里参观。其中，宽巷子以老成都的生活体验为主，窄巷子里主要是饭馆、茶馆、咖啡馆和酒吧，井巷子有一道文化墙。

成都的宽窄巷子是刚来成都的游客最喜欢去的地方。在这里可以感受到老成都的民俗，在巷子里面走走，好像走进了历史、回到了过去。

成都市周围还有一些特色古镇和古文化街，包括洛带古镇、黄龙溪古镇、街子古镇、安仁古镇等。每个古镇都各有特点。拿洛带古镇来说，据说三国时期（220 — 280 年）就有了洛带古镇，古镇的很多村

① 井　　jǐng
② 组 成　zǔchéng
③ 街 道　jiēdào
④ 商 业　shāngyè
⑤ 镇　　zhèn
⑥ 黄龙溪　Huánglóngxī
⑦ 街 子　Jiē zi
⑧ 安 仁　Ān rén
⑨ 据 说　jùshuō

⑩时　期　shíqī
⑪洛　带　Luòdài
⑫客　家　Kèjiā
⑬土　楼　tǔlóu
⑭建　筑　jiànzhù

民是客家人，很多房子是清代客家土楼样式的建筑，附近还有一段小长城，周末可以约朋友一起爬爬小长城。其他的古镇都有历史上留下来的老街、绿树、河水，像山水画一样。当然，除了古老的建筑，成都也有现代的一面。

【五】天府广场—春熙路

①正　　　zhèng
②像　　　xiàng
③象　征　xiàngzhēng
④名　片　míngpiàn
⑤侧　　　cè
⑥四川科技馆
　Sìchuān Kējìguǎn
⑦成都博物馆
　Chéngdū Bówùguǎn
⑧锦城艺术宫
　Jǐnchéng Yìshùgōng
⑨喷　泉　pēnquán
⑩太阳神鸟
　tàiyáng shénniǎo
⑪太　极　Tàijí
⑫图　案　tú àn

　　天府广场位于成都市区的中心。广场的正北方有高30米的毛主席像，这里是成都甚至整个四川的象征，是成都的城市名片。

　　天府广场北侧是四川科技馆，西侧是成都博物馆，南侧有天府书城和城市之心，东侧是锦城艺术宫。广场里的音乐喷泉和太阳神鸟很漂亮。从高处看天府广场，会看到一个太极的图案。天府广场是地铁的换乘车站，也是整个成都交通的中心点。

大萌：
　　看完了天府广场，我们去春熙路吧！

江一华：
　　我听说过春熙路，它是成都最著名的商业街。

文小西：
　　我们怎么去？

大萌：

从天府广场往东走 15 分钟就可以到。春熙路是成都最古老的商业街之一，是"中国商业街排行榜"上的第三名。

文小西：

哇，一路上这么多人，路边都是商店，很热闹。

大萌：

周末的时候更热闹，有时候路上全是人挤在一起。春熙路旁边新修了 IFS（国际金融中心）和太古里，我们往那边走。

文小西：

看！那里有一只熊猫在爬楼呢。

大萌：

IFS 楼顶的熊猫现在成了新的景点，来成都的人都会去楼顶和这只熊猫拍个照。

江一华：

看，前面停着很多熊猫交通车，真可爱。我们坐过的景点交通车也在旁边。

大萌：

再往前面走一点儿，就到太古里了，这里是目前成都最潮的购物中心。

⑬换 乘　huànchéng
⑭排行榜　páihángbǎng
⑮热 闹　rènao
⑯挤　　　jǐ
⑰风 格　fēnggé
⑱仔 细　zǐxì
⑲名 牌　míngpái
⑳节 奏　jiézòu
㉑精 致　jīngzhì
㉒悠 闲　yōuxián
㉓独 特　dútè

江一华：

　这里的房子都不高，造型看起来很有四川传统民居的风格。

文小西：

　不过仔细一看，都是些奢侈品商店。

大　萌：

　是的，旁边还有大慈寺，商业和历史的相遇让太古里显得既传统又现代。

文小西：

　周围都是高楼，这里的房子却只有两三层，走在里面觉得很舒服。

大　萌：

　四川人喜欢慢生活，太古里里面有名牌商店、精致的餐馆，也有悠闲的茶馆和咖啡馆，地下一楼还有超市和电影院。附近也有一些便宜、时尚的小店，还有很多特色餐馆。

文小西：

　在热闹的城市中心也有"慢生活"，这让我觉得成都和其他的大城市不一样，有独特的美和生活方式。

春熙路，得名于老子《道德经》。它是1924年修建成的，是成都的商业中心。在春熙路上不仅有大大小小的商店，而且能看到旧时的建筑和春熙路的老照片，还有很多成都有名的小吃店，是成都人和外地人必须到的成都景点之一。太古里和IFS就在春熙路，现在是成都春熙路的新地标。

㉔ 老　子　Lǎozǐ
㉕ 道德经　dàodéjīng
㉖ 地　标　dìbiāo

【六】旧厂房与新艺术——成都东郊记忆公园

20世纪50年代到60年代，成都东门有国家重要的工厂，那里留下了一代成都人的记忆，也留下了那个年代的中国式工厂文化。后来，成都市把这些老工厂与新的艺术结合起来，创造出了独特的"记忆旅游""工业旅游"。在成都，这样旧房新用的文化创意园大概有5个，其中最有名的是东郊记忆公园。2009年，成都市开始改造东郊记忆公园，2011年向外界开放。在东郊记忆公园人们可以看到中国式的

① 世　纪　shìjì
② 年　代　niándài
③ 记　忆　jìyì
④ 结　合　jiéhé
⑤ 工　业　gōngyè
⑥ 创　意　chuàngyì
⑦ 改　造　gǎizào

⑧话　剧　huàjù
⑨欣　赏　xīnshǎng
⑩展　览　zhǎnlǎn

老厂房，还可以欣赏到新的艺术创作、现代艺术展览、音乐节和话剧等。有人把东郊记忆公园叫作"中国的伦敦西区"，它也被人民网评为"首批中国文化旅游新地标"。

　　走在公园里除了能够看到最新的演出，还可以感受城市的变化、走进来自工业的记忆。

【七】成都大熊猫研究基地

①至　少　zhìshǎo
②保　护　bǎohù
③度　　　dù
④树　林　shùlín
⑤竹　子　zhúzi
⑥作　为　zuòwéi
⑦礼　物　lǐwù
⑧动物园　dòngwùyuán
⑨出　租　chūzū
⑩短　期　duǎnqī
⑪借　展　jièzhǎn
⑫科　研　kēyán
⑬交　流　jiāoliú
⑭和　平　hépíng
⑮环　境　huánjìng
⑯习　惯　xíguàn

　　大熊猫在地球上至少生活了 800 万年，它是中国特有的保护动物，全世界 80% 的熊猫都生活在四川。它们在 20 度以下的树林里生活，大部分时间都在睡觉，有时候也会爬树、吃竹子和苹果。它们动作很慢，十分可爱。20 世纪 50 年代，中国开始向其他国家赠送大熊猫作为礼物。80 年代之后，中国开始向国外动物园出租大熊猫。大熊猫走向世界经历了赠送、短期借展、科研交流的漫长岁月，大熊猫们去了不同的国家，带去了和平和快乐。

（在大熊猫研究基地）

文小西：

　　我今天学到了很多。现在对我来说，大熊猫不只是一个可爱的中国"国宝"了，我知道了它生活的环境、它的生活习惯，真有意思。

大 萌：

每年熊猫基地的工作人员都会办培训班，宣传保护动物的知识，而且大熊猫移动博物馆还到学校里去，让孩子们了解大熊猫，保护大熊猫。

江 一华：

我们也可以参加吗？

大 萌：

当然可以，你和小西都可以申请当"大熊猫科普志愿者"，给来自世界各国的人们讲讲大熊猫，让更多的人学习怎么保护大熊猫、保护环境。

⑰办　　bàn
⑱街　　jiē
⑲培训班　péixùnbān
⑳宣传　xuānchuán
㉑知识　zhīshi
㉒移动　yídòng
㉓参加　cānjiā
㉔申请　shēnqǐng
㉕科普　kēpǔ
㉖志愿者　zhìyuànzhě
㉗大熊猫研究基地
　Dàxióngmāo Yánjiū Jīdì
㉘开展　kāizhǎn
㉙合作　hézuò
㉚繁育　fǎnyù

　　成都大熊猫繁育研究基地在成都市成华区外北熊猫大道 1375 号，是世界著名的大熊猫研究基地。游客在这里可以看到大熊猫的生活情况、了解有关大熊猫的知识。基地主要做大熊猫科学研究、保护繁育、教育旅游、熊猫文化的工作。另外，这里还与很多国家开展交流和合作，一起保护大熊猫。

Jiang Yihua: Da Meng, today is the first day of Xiaoxi and me to arrive in Chengdu. Where will you take us to have some fun?

Da Meng: Chengdu City' s famous attractions are: Tianfu Square, Chunxi Road, Du Fu Thatched Cottage, Kuanzhai Alley, Wuhou Temple, Jinli as well as many parks. Where do you want to go?

Xiaoxi: To a place with few people, ideally one with delicious food.

Da Meng: We' ll go to Du Fu Thatched Cottage first, then to Wuhou Temple and Jinli today. Tomorrow we' ll go to the city center, Tianfu Square, Chunxi Road and Kuanzhai Alley.

Part 1 【Du Fu Thatched Cottage】

Jiang Yihua: Du Fu Thatched Cottage is stunning! These trees are both tall and big, the flowers beautiful and there is also this small river with really clean water.

Da Meng: Look! That hut in front is Du Fu's home.

Wen Xiaoxi: Da Meng, isn't Du Fu a famous poet? Why is his house so old and so small? It looks quite shabby!

Da Meng: This is a good question. At that time, Du Fu was poor and not all that successful in his work – he had no money. Even this hut was built through the help of a friend. The house we're now looking at was later rebuilt.

Jiang Yihua: How would you go about rebuilding, though? How do you know what it originally looked like?

Da Meng: Du Fu wrote a lot of poems. From them, we can imagine what his hut looked like and then how it was built.

Wen Xiaoxi: How long did Du Fu live in this cottage and how many poems did he write?

Da Meng: Du Fu lived there for almost four years in total and wrote more than 240 poems. During his stay, he planted his own flowers. One of his poems describes Chengdu's spring rain – it is one beautiful piece of art. There is one verse that means, "After a night of spring rain, flowers can be seen sprinkled with rain water, and the City of the Brocade Officer appears as a world of flowers – absolutely gorgeous."

Jiang Yihua: Da Meng, what verse is that, could you help me write it down?

Da Meng: The verse is, "Come dawn, we'll see splashes of wet red – The flowers in the City of the Brocade Officer, weighed down with rain". "City of the Brocade Officer" is an alternative name for Chengdu.

Jiang Yihua: Thank you. After we're back, I' ll look up Du Fu on the Internet tonight and learn more about this great poet.

Du Fu Thatched Cottage is in the west of Chengdu and is Tang dynasty poet Du Fu's home. Du Fu is"The Saint of Poems"and his poems are piece of history that reflected his times. Although he lived in Chengdu for merely four years, he wrote many famous poems here. If you come to Chengdu, you absolutely must go to Du Fu Thatched Cottage and see it for yourself.

Part 2 【Wuhou Temple】

Da Meng: The combo ticket for Chengdu's tourist attractions is both really cheap and convenient. It took us only half an hour from Du Fu Thatched Cottage to Wuhou Ci. The bus was particularly comfortable and there was also a free introduction by a tour guide.

Jiang Yihua: Right! Let's take the same bus when we go to the other attractions!

Wen Xiaoxi: "Wuhou" refers to Zhuge Liang, but what does" 祠 "mean?

Da Meng: You've been studying Chinese characters, right? What does " 礻 " mean?

Jiang Yihua: Our teacher told us and drew the character, it looks like a person worshipping a god or someone who passed away, right?

Da Meng: Right. This" 祠 "refers to place where the dead are commemorated.

Wen Xiaoxi: Oh, I get it!"Wuhou Ci"is the place where Zhuge Liang is commemorated.

Da Meng: "Wuhou Ci"isn't only for the commemoration of Zhuge Liang; it was also built in remembrance of Liu Bei. Let's get going, I'll tell you more during our visit.

Jiang Yihua: I'm guessing the person holding the feather fan is Zhuge Liang?

Da Meng: Correct. Further ahead is "Hui Ling", the place for commemoration of Liu Bei.

Wuhou Temple is in the south of Chengdu and consists of three parts: the first one is the Cultural Heritage Protection Area, mainly including Han Zhaolie Temple, Wuhou Temple, Hui Ling and Sanyi Temple; the second is the Cultural Experience Area; and the third one is the Jinli Folk Area. Here, you can learn more about the history of the State Shu, which is one of the"Three Kingdoms", see some ancient Chinese calligraphic arts as well as many traditional handicrafts from Chengdu, and enjoy a wide range of Chengdu's snacks.

Part 3 【Ancient Cultural Streets and Ancient Towns in Chengdu】

Da Meng: Now that we've seen Wuhou Temple, we'll go to the Jinli Ancient Street nearby. Jinli may be newly built, but you can still experience the Three Kingdoms and traditional Chengdu culture.

Jiang Yihua: Look, the stalls over there sell souvenirs. I' m going to buy some for my family and friends!

Wen Xiaoxi: Wow, what is this smell? Smells delicious!

Da Meng: There is a snack street in front where they only sell Chengdu snacks.

Wen Xiaoxi: Jinli is really cool! Not only can you buy a lot of traditional Chengdu souvenirs, but also so many delicious Chengdu snacks.

Da Meng: True. Chengdu may have several Ancient Cultural Streets, but each cultural street has its own history and characteristics. Jinli, for example, is an ancient street based on the Three Kingdoms culture. The theme of Kuanzhai Alley is the Qing Dynasty culture. They're all quite distinctive and worth a look.

Part 4 【Kuanzhai Alley】

Kuanzhai Alley is made up of the three alleys Kuan, Zhai and Jing, and is an ancient street left over by the Qing dynasty. Kuanzhai Alley nowadays has become a commercial street that every day countless tourists come to visit. With the Old Chengdu living experience as its theme, Zhai Alley mainly houses restaurants, teahouses, cafes and bars, while Jing Alley features a cultural wall.

Chengdu's Kuanzhai Alley is the favorite place of tourists who just arrived in Chengdu. Here, you can experience the Old Chengdu folk customs. Strolling Kuan Alley is like entering a moment of history, going back to the past.

There are also some characteristic ancient towns and ancient cultural streets around Chengdu, including Luodai Ancient Town, Jiezi Ancient Town, Anren Ancient Town and so on. Each town is special in its own way. Luodai, for example, is said to have existed during the Three Kingdoms era (220-280). Many inhabitants of these ancient towns are Hakka and many of their dwellings are built in the Qing Dynasty tulou style. There is also a mini great wall nearby, which you can climb with your friends together at the weekend. Other ancient towns feature old streets, trees and rivers passed down by history and are reminiscent of landscape paintings. Of course, apart from these ancient towns, Chengdu also has a modern side.

Part 5 【Tianfu Square – Chunxi Road】

Tianfu Square is located in the center of Chengdu City. There is a 30-meter-high Mao Zedong statue directly in the north of Tianfu Square. It is the symbol of Chengdu and even Sichuan as a whole; it is the city's figurehead.

To the north of Tianfu Square lies the Sichuan Science and Technology Museum. The Chengdu Museum can be found to the west, Tianfu Bookstore and the Heart of the City to the south, and Jincheng Art Palace to the east. The square's musical fountain and the Golden Sun Bird are gorgeous. Standing atop a high place, you can see a Taiji pattern on the square. Tianfu Square is a subway transfer station and also the transport center of the entire city.

Da Meng: Now that we've had a look around the Tianfu Square, let's go to Chunxi Road!

Jiang Yihua: I've heard about Chunxi Road. It's Chengdu's most famous commercial street.

Wen Xiaoxi: How do we get there?

Da Meng: Simply go east from Tianfu Square for 15 minutes and you'll be there. Chunxi Road is one of the oldest shopping streets in Chengdu, and places third on " China's Commercial Streets Ranking".

Wen Xiaoxi: Wow, there are so many people on the road, and the roadsides are full of stores. What a lively place!

Da Meng: It is even livelier during the weekend. Sometimes the roads are absolutely packed. Next to Chunxi Road is the newly built IFS (International Finance Square) and Taikoo Li. Let's go over there.

Wen Xiaoxi: Look! There is a panda climbing atop the building.

Da Meng: The panda on the top of the IFS has become a new attraction. Those who come to Chengdu will go to the roof and take a picture with this panda.

Jiang Yihua: Look, there are a lot of panda buses in the front. They look so cute! The bus we take to see the attractions is also next to them.

Da Meng: Go a bit further ahead and we'll arrive at Taikoo Li. It is the latest shopping mall.

Jiang Yihua: The buildings here aren't all that tall and their style looks traditional Sichuanese.

Wen Xiaoxi: But if you take a closer look, these are all expensive brand-name stores.

Da Meng: Yes, and Daci Temple is nearby. Business and history meet and make Taikoo Li both traditional and modern.

Wen Xiaoxi: The surrounding buildings are tall, while these here are only two or three stocks tall. Walking around here makes me feel comfortable.

Da Meng: The Sichuanese like their slow-paced lives and hope that life doesn't get hectic. Inside Taikoo Li are brand-name stores, fine restaurants, and also relaxing teahouses and cafes. There are also supermarkets and movie theaters underground. Some cheap, stylish shops are nearby as well as many specialty restaurants.

Wen Xiaoxi: Slow-paced life amidst the bustling city center – this makes me think that Chengdu is unlike other big cities; it has its own unique beauty.

Chunxi Road got its name from Laozi's "Daodejing". It was built in 1924 and is Chengdu's commercial center. There are not only all kinds of large and small stores, but also old architectures and old pictures of Chunxi Road to be seen, and even a lot of famous Chengdu snack bars. It is one of Chengdu's must-go places for locals and non-locals alike. Taikoo Li and IFS are located on Chunxi Road, which are now the new landmarks of Chengdu's Chunxi Road.

Part 6 【Old Factories and New Art – Chengdu Eastern Suburb Memory Park】

From the 1950s to the 1960s, important national factories and enterprises were all located at Chengdu's east gate, where the memories of one generation of Chengdu people and that era's Chinese factory culture were left behind. Later, Chengdu combined these old factories with new art forms to create unique forms of "nostalgia tourism" and "industrial tourism". In Chengdu, there are about 5 of these old factories reused as cultural and creative parks, the most famous being the Eastern Suburb Memory Park. In 2009, Chengdu started to reform the memory park in the eastern suburb and opened it to the public in 2011. In the

Eastern Suburb Memory Park, you can see old Chinese factories and also enjoy the creation of new art, modern painting exhibitions, music festivals and drama. Some call the Eastern Suburb Memory Park "China's West End". It has been rated as "China's first batch of new landmarks in cultural tourism"by people. Strolling around the park not only lets you see the latest shows, but also enables you to experience the changes that the city has undergone and relieve the memories from an industrial time gone by.

Part 7 【 Chengdu Research Base of Giant Panda Breeding 】

Giant pandas have lived on the earth for at least 8 million years. They are endemic to China and 80% of the world's population lives in Sichuan. They live in the woods below 20 degrees Celsius, sleep most of the time, sometimes climb trees and eat bamboo and apples. They are slow and cute. In the 1950s, China began giving away pandas to other countries as gifts. After the 1980s, China started to rent giant pandas to foreign zoos. The giant pandas have gone through long years of being gifts, short-term loan exhibitions and objects of scientific exchanges. They have been to different countries and brought peace and happiness.

(At the Giant Panda Research Base)

Wen Xiaoxi: I learnt a lot today. To me, the giant panda isn't just a lovely Chinese "national treasure". I learnt about its living environment and habits. So fascinating!

Da Meng: Every year, the panda base staff will organize training courses to spread facts about animal protection and the Giant Panda Moving Museum visits schools to let children learn about the giant panda and its protection.

Jiang Yihua: Can we join, too?

Da Meng: Of course you can. Both you and Xiaoxi can apply as "Giant Panda Awareness Raiser", teaching all things about giant pandas to people from all over the world and teach them how to protect giant pandas and the environment.

The Chengdu Research Base of Giant Panda Breeding in Chenghua District, No. 1375 North Panda Avenue, Chengdu, is a world-famous giant panda research base. Here, visitors can see how pandas live and learn more about them. The base's main tasks are the scientific research of giant pandas, protection, breeding, education, tourism and panda culture. In addition, it also carries out exchange and cooperation programs with many countries, to protect the giant panda together.

词 语

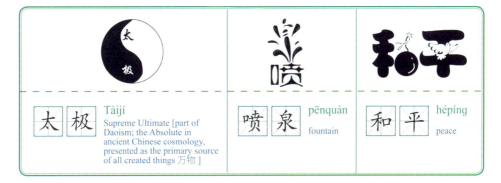

太 极	Tàijí Supreme Ultimate [part of Daoism; the Absolute in ancient Chinese cosmology, presented as the primary source of all created things 万物]	喷 泉	pēnquán fountain	和 平	hépíng peace

zuì hǎo 最 好	best; it would be best	gān jìng 干 净	clean
lián 连	(used correlatively with "也", "都", etc.)even	máo wū 茅 屋	hut
zhù míng 著 名	famous	shī rén 诗 人	poet
shùn lì 顺 利	smooth; successful; without a hitch	hòu lái 后 来	afterwards; later
chóng xīn 重 新	again	xiǎngxiàng 想 象	imagine

jǐng diǎn 景 点	scenic spot; place of interest; attraction
tào piào 套 票	admission package; ticket combo
miǎn fèi 免 费	free of charge
bài shén 拜 神	pray to God/ the gods; worship
yǔ máo 羽 毛	feather; plume
yí chǎn 遗 产	legacy; inheritance; heritage
tǐ yàn 体 验	experience for oneself
páng biān 旁 边	nearby

cān guān 参 观	visit; have a look around
dǎo yóu 导 游	tourist guide
jiè shào 介 绍	introduce
jì niàn 纪 念	commemorate; remember
shàn zi 扇 子	fan
qū 区	area; zone
mín sú 民 俗	folk custom
xiǎo tān 小 摊	stall

jì niàn pǐn 纪 念 品	souvenir
xiāng 香	fragrant; aromatic; savory; tasty
zhǔ tí 主 题	main body/part
jǐng 井	well
jiē dào 街 道	street; residential district
zhèn 镇	town
shí qī 时 期	(particular) period
zhèng 正	situated in the middle (opp. 侧 , 偏)

wèi dào 味 道	taste; flavor
tè sè 特 色	characteristic; distinguishing feature (or quality)
zhí dé 值 得	worth (doing sth.)
zǔ chéng 组 成	form; make up; compose
shāng yè 商 业	commerce; trade; business
jù shuō 据 说	it is said; they say; allegedly
jiàn zhù 建 筑	building; structure; architecture
xiàng 像	statue

míng piàn 名 片	visiting/calling/name/ business card; signature…; flagship; figurehead
tú àn 图 案	pattern; design/
huàn chéng 换 乘	transfer; change (to another public conveyance)
rè nao 热 闹	lively; bustling
zǐ xì 仔 细	attentive; careful
jié zòu 节 奏	rhythm; pace
yōu xián 悠 闲	leisurely
dì biāo 地 标	landmark

xiàng zhēng 象 征	symbol; symbolize
cè 侧	side
pái háng bǎng 排 行 榜	leaderboard; ranking
jǐ 挤	crowd; pack
míng pái 名 牌	famous brand
jīng zhì 精 致	fine; exquisite; delicate
dú tè 独 特	unique; distinctive
shì jì 世 纪	century

nián dài 年 代	time
jié hé 结 合	combine; unite; integrate
chuàng yì 创 意	creativity; innovation; create a new concept; innovate
huà jù 话 剧	modern drama; stage play
zhǎn lǎn 展 览	put on display; exhibit; show
zhì shǎo 至 少	at least
dù 度	(unit of measurement for angles, temperature, etc.) degree
zuò wéi 作 为	in the capacity (or character, role) of; as

jì yì 记 忆	memory
gōng yè 工 业	industry
gǎi zào 改 造	transform
xīn shǎng 欣 赏	enjoy
bǎo hù 保 护	protect; safeguard
shù lín 树 林	woods; forest
zhú zi 竹 子	bamboo
lǐ wù 礼 物	gift; present

chū zū 出 租	rent
jiè zhǎn 借 展	(loan) exhibition; exhibit loaned (objects, animals…)
jiāo liú 交 流	exchange
xí guàn 习 惯	habit
péi xùn bān 培 训 班	training course
zhī shi 知 识	knowledge
cān jiā 参 加	join
kē pǔ 科 普	popularization of science

dòng wù yuán 动 物 园	zoo
duǎn qī 短 期	short-term; short duration
kē yán 科 研	scientific research
huán jìng 环 境	environment
bàn 办	do; manage; run; set up
xuān chuán 宣 传	propagate; spread (information)
yí dòng 移 动	mobile
shēn qǐng 申 请	apply

kāi zhǎn 开 展	launch; develop; carry out	zhì yuàn zhě 志 愿 者	volunteer
fán yù 繁 育	breed	hé zuò 合 作	cooperate; work together; collaborate

专 有 名 词

1. 天府广场 /Tiānfǔ Guǎngchǎng / Tianfu Square

2. 锦官城 / Jǐnguān chéng / City of the Brocade Officer

3. 汉昭烈庙 /Hàn Zhāoliè Miào / Zhaolie Temple of Han

4. 惠陵 / Huì líng / Hui Ling

5. 三义庙 / Sān yì Miào / Sanyi Temple

6. 蜀国 / Shǔ guó / State of Shu

7. 洛带 / Luò dài / Luodai

8. 街子 / Jiē zi / Jiezi

9. 黄龙溪 / Huáng lóng xī / Huanglongxi

10. 安仁 / Ān rén / Anren

11. 太阳神鸟　　/ Tàiyáng Shénniǎo / the Golden Sun Bird

12. 四川科技馆　/ Sìchuān Kējìguǎn / Sichuan Science and Technology Museum (includes airplanes, flying saucers, 3D movies, robots and interactive model rockets)

13. 成都博物馆　/ Chéngdū Bówùguǎn / Chengdu Museum

14. 锦城艺术宫　/ Jǐnchéng Yìshùgōng /Jincheng Art Palace (houses an amphitheater showing concerts, ballets, operas and dramas)

15. 道德经　　　/ Dàodé Jīng / Daodejing or Tao Te Ching; The Classic of the Virtue of the Tao; by Laozi

16. 老子　　　　/ Lǎozǐ / Laozi or Lao-tzu, reverent term of address for Li Er; Chinese philosopher of the late Spring and Autumn period (ca. 500 BC) and founder of Taoism; alternative name for the sacred book of Taoism, the Daodejing

17. 大熊猫研究基地 / Dàxíónmāo Yánjiū Jīdì /Chengdu Research Base of Giant Panda Breeding

语言点

1. 又……又……　　　　2. 连……也……

3. 动词 + "一" + 动词　　4. 不只……也……

5. 一边……一边……　　　6. 好 + 几 / 多

7. 以……为……   8. 据说……

9. ……之一   10. 是……的

11. 后来   12. 被……评为……

13. 虽然……但是……

思 考

1. 你最喜欢的成都市内景点是什么？为什么？

2. 你喜欢历史的景点还是现代的？为什么？

第三课
Lesson 3

【都江堰—青城山景区】

【Dujiangyan – Mt. Qingcheng Scenic Area】

来到成都除了要看市内有名的景点，还值得去逛逛的是都江堰风景区。都江堰市位于成都的西北边，都江堰景区主要有青城山和都江堰水利工程两个景点，这两个景点都是"世界文化遗产"。

【一】青城山

① 直通车 zhítōngchē
② 动 车 dòngchē
③ 古 镇 gǔzhèn

大 萌：

小西、一华，你们快点儿，我们今天得去参观非常重要的地方——青城山和都江堰，得早点儿出发。

江 一华：

知道啦，大萌。对了，我昨天晚上查了一下都江堰，离成都市有点儿远，我们怎么去呢？打出租车去很贵吧？

大 萌：

可以在市中心坐景点直通车，也可以坐动车去。从成都坐动车到青城山，差不多要 40 分钟。我已经买好动车票了，8:30 出发，现在去火车站还来得及。

文 小西：

青城山为什么重要呢？

大 萌：

　青城山分前山和后山，是有名的道教名山。前山有很多道教建筑，后山有山有水有古镇，风景很美。

文 小西：

　那我们今天去前山还是后山？

大 萌：

　今天去前山，我们从青城山火车站坐公共汽车到前山只要 10 分钟。

（到青城山了）

大 萌：

　青城前山到了。你们想爬上去还是坐缆车上去？

江 一华：

　青城山不高，我们可以慢慢走上去，一边走一边看风景，然后再坐缆车下山，怎么样？

文 小西：

　好啊！

① 缆　车　lǎnchē
② 发源地　fāyuándì
③ 道　教　Dàojiào
④ 观　　Guàn
⑤ 宫　　Gōng
⑥ 佛　教　Fójiào
⑦ 隋　　Suí
⑧ 休　息　xiūxi

大 萌：

青城山是中国道教的发源地之一，已经有两千多年的历史了。道教的建筑我们一般叫"观"或者"宫"，比如我们去过的"青羊宫"，而佛教的建筑一般叫"寺"，比如，我们去过的"大慈寺"。

江—华：

大萌，这些建筑是什么时候修的呢？

大 萌：

最早的大概是在隋唐时期修的，后来人们不断重修，所以我们看到有的地方新，有的地方旧。

大 萌：

青城山看完以后，下一站我们去都江堰。

江—华、文小西：

好，那我们休息一下就下山吧。

【二】都江堰水利工程

大 萌：

前面就是都江堰水利工程了，都江堰不仅是世界闻名的中国古代水利工程，也是著名的风景区。

① 水 利　shuǐlì
② 工 程　gōngchéng
③ 闻 名　wénmíng
④ 图 片　túpiàn
⑤ 工 具　gōngjù
⑥ 好 奇　hàoqí
⑦ 伟 大　wěidà
⑧ 神 奇　shénqí

文小西：
这里有多长时间的历史了？

大萌：
都江堰水利工程是 2 300 多年前修建的，我们先看"二王庙"，这是纪念李冰和他儿子的地方。你们看，这个人是李冰，都江堰就是他和他的儿子带着人们修的。

文小西：
这些石牛是做什么的呢？

大萌：
这些石牛是当时用来测水的高度的，这里还有介绍他们怎么修水利工程的图片和他们使用的工具。

江一华：
很好奇他们当时是怎么修的，而且过了两千多年还能用，太伟大了！

大萌：
接下来再带你们去看看都江堰神奇的地方：鱼嘴、飞沙堰和宝瓶口。你们看，"鱼嘴"把江分成两部分，"外江"和"内江"。"内江"的水主要用来给农田浇水。

文 小西：

　这是"飞沙堰"吧，除了石头和沙子以外，没有别的东西呀。

大 萌：

　你可不要小看它，它非常重要。如果"内江"的水太多、对农田有害，多的水就会从"飞沙堰"流到"外江"去，这样就可以控制流入宝瓶口的水量，成都就不会有洪水。

江 一华：

　这里为什么叫飞沙堰？是因为可以让沙飞出去吗？

⑨鱼嘴　　yúzuǐ
⑩浇　　　jiāo
⑪害　　　hài
⑫飞沙堰　Fēishā Yàn
⑬控制　　kòngzhì
⑭宝瓶口　Bǎopíng Kǒu
⑮洪水　　hóngshuǐ
⑯地形　　dìxíng
⑰堵　　　dǔ
⑱干旱　　gānhàn
⑲遗产　　yíchǎn

大萌：

是的，由于地形原因，"飞沙堰"可以把水里的泥沙、石头跟河水分开，不让这些泥沙和石头堵住"内江"进入成都的路。

文小西：

大萌，那边怎么有那么多人呀？他们在看什么呀？

大萌：

那里就是"宝瓶口"，是"内江"进成都的入口，它像一个瓶口，水从这个小小的瓶口慢慢流入成都，所以，成都不会干旱也不会有大洪水。

江一华：

都江堰真是太重要了，它给成都带来了这么多好处。

大萌：

自从都江堰修好以后，成都成了著名的"天府之国"。青城山和都江堰水利工程都是"世界文化遗产"，除了风景好，也有非常重要的意义。

When you come to Chengdu, the Dujiangyan Scenic Area is also worth a visit apart from the famous attractions within the city. Dujiangyan is located to the northwest of Chengdu and mainly consists of Mt. Qingcheng and the Dujiangyan Water Conservancy Project. These two areas are parts of the "World Heritage".

Part 1 【 Mt. Qingcheng 】

Da Meng: Xiaoxi, Yihua, hurry up! We must go to very important places today: Mt. Qingcheng and Dujiangyan. We'll have to set out early.

Jiang Yihua: Got it, Da Meng! By the way, I looked Dujiangyan up last night; it's a bit far from Chengdu. How do we get there? Taking a taxi would be expensive, wouldn't it?

Da Meng: You can take the sightseeing bus in the city center or the high-speed train there. Going from Chengdu to Mt. Qingcheng first takes about forty minutes. I've already bought the train tickets. The train leaves at 8:30 am. If we go right now, we'll make it in time.

Wen Xiaoxi: Why is Mt. Qingcheng important?

Da Meng: Mt. Qingcheng is made up of its front and back mountains and is a famous Daoist mountain. The front mountain has many Daoist buildings, while the back mountain has mountains, water and ancient towns. Its scenery is beautiful.

Wen Xiaoxi: So, are we going to the front or back mountain today?

Da Meng: We'll go to the front mountain today. Taking the bus from Mt. Qingcheng railway station to the front mountain only takes ten minutes.
(They arrived at Mt. Qingcheng.)

Da Meng: We've arrived at the front mountain of Mt. Qingcheng. Do you want to hike or take the cable car to the top?

Jiang Yihua: Mt. Qingcheng isn't tall; we can slowly walk our way up. We'll enjoy the scenery while we walk and then take cable car back down. What about it?

Wen Xiaoxi: I'm all for it!

Da Meng: Mt. Qingcheng is one of the cradles of Chinese Daoism and has a history of more than two thousand years. We generally call Daoist buildings "monasteries" or "palaces", for example "Qingyang Palace", which we visited. For Buddhist buildings, on the other hand, we usually call them "temples", for example , "Daci Temple", which we also visited.

Jiang Yihua: Da Meng, when were these buildings built?

Da Meng: The earliest one probably in the Sui and Tang Dynasties. Later, they were constantly rebuilt and renovated, so some of them are new, and some of them are old.

Wen Xiaoxi: After we've seen Mt. Qingcheng, our next stop will be Dujiangyan, right ?

Da Meng: All right. Let's take a break and make our way down.

Part 2 【Dujiangyan Water Conservancy Project】

Da Meng: In front is the Dujiangyan Water Conservancy Project. Not only is it a world-famous ancient Chinese water conservancy project, Dujiangyan is also a famous scenic spot.

Wen Xiaoxi: How long is its history?

Da Meng: Dujiangyan was built 2,300 years ago. We'll first visit Erwang Temple, where Li Bing and his son are commemorated. Look, this person is Li Bing. It was under his and his son's guidance that Dujiangyan was built.

Wen Xiaoxi: What are these bulls doing?

Da Meng: These stone bulls were used to measure the water height at that time. Here are also pictures of how they built the conservancy project and of the tools they used.

Jiang Yihua: I'm curious about how they went about construction. Also, it can still be used after more than 2,000 years, amazing!

Da Meng: Next, I'll take you to the places where the magic happens: the"fish mouth", the "flying sand weir" and the "mouth of the treasure bottle". Look, the fish mouth splits the river into two: the "outer river" and the "inner river". The inner river is mainly used to water the farmland.

Wen Xiaoxi: I guess this is the "flying sand weir". There's nothing to be seen except stone and sand.

Da Meng: Don't sell it short. It's very important. If the inner river carries too much water and is harmful to the farmland, the excess water will flow from the flying sand weir to the outer river. In this way, the water flowing into the mouth of the treasure bottle can be controlled and Chengdu won't be flooded.

Jiang Yihua: Why is it called "flying sand weir"? Is it because it can make sand fly away?

Da Meng: Yes. Because of the terrain, the weir can separate the silt and stones from the water and stop them from blocking the inner river to flow into Chengdu.

Wen Xiaoxi: Da Meng, there are so many people over there; what're they looking at?

Da Meng: The mouth of the treasure bottle is over there, which is the inner river's point of entry into Chengdu. The mouth looks like that of a bottle, from which the water flows slowly into Chengdu. As a result, Chengdu doesn't suffer from droughts or great floods.

Jiang Yihua: Dujiangyan is extremely important and has brought so many benefits to Chengdu.

Da Meng: After Dujiangyan's construction was finished, Chengdu became the famous "Land of Plenty". Mt. Qingcheng and the Dujiangyan Water Conservancy Project are parts of the "world cultural heritage". Apart from their beautiful scenery, they also play a significant role.

词语

| 浇 | jiāo
irrigate; water | 控 制 | kòngzhi
control | 堵 | dǔ
stop up; block up |

zhí tōng chē 直 通 车	through bus/ train
gǔ zhèn 古 镇	ancient town
fā yuán dì 发 源 地	cradle
shuǐ lì 水 利	water conserv- ancy (project); irrigation works
wén míng 闻 名	well-known; famous; renowned

dòng chē 动 车	CRH (China Railway Highspeed) train
lǎn chē 缆 车	cable car
xiū xi 休 息	take a break
gōng chéng 工 程	project; program; engineering
tú piàn 图 片	picture

gōng jù 工 具	tool
wěi dà 伟 大	great; grand; worthy of the greatest admiration; important (contribution…)
hài 害	harm
gān hàn 干 旱	drought

hào qí 好 奇	curious
shén qí 神 奇	magical; mystical; miraculous; effective and startling
hóng shuǐ 洪 水	flood
dì xíng 地 形	terrain

专 有 名 词

1. 隋 / Suí / Sui Dynasty (581-617)

2. 鱼嘴 / Yú Zuǐ / fish mouth

3. 飞沙堰 / Fēishā Yàn / flying sand weir

4. 宝瓶口 / Bǎopíng Kǒu / mouth of the treasure bottle

语言点

1. 来得及　　　　　　2. 而
3. 把……V.+ 成……　　4. 自从……以后

思考

1. 你有宗教信仰吗？你怎样理解佛教和道教？
2. 在你的国家有没有水利工程？如果有的话，请介绍一下。

第四课 【成都的博物馆】
Lesson 4 【Museums in Chengdu】

如果你想真正了解一个城市，不只要去一些街道，不只要吃一点小吃、逛一些景点，还要去这个城市的博物馆。在博物馆里，我们不仅能了解这个城市的历史，还能了解许多有趣的知识。成都是中国古代文明的重要起源中心之一，成都的博物馆数量全国第一。走进成都的博物馆，就像走进了历史，你会和历史人物说话。博物馆不仅可以让人们更好地了解成都的过去，也可以看到成都的现在和未来。

① 文 明　　wénmíng
② 起 源　　qǐyuán
③ 人 物　　rénwù
④ 未 来　　wèilái

【一】四川博物院

大萌：
一华、小西，今天我们去四川博物院怎么样？

文小西：
好，四川博物院在哪儿？远吗？

大萌：
一点儿都不远。咱们现在从学校出发，坐地铁或公共汽车三站就到了。

（在四川博物院）

① 少 数　　hǎoshù
② 民 族　　mínzú
③ 藏 族　　Zàngzú
④ 彝 族　　Yízú
⑤ 羌 族　　Qiāngzú
⑥ 综 合　　zōnghé
⑦ 厅　　　tīng
⑧ 文 物　　wénwù
⑨ 展 馆　　zhǎnguǎn
⑩ 地 址　　dìzhǐ
⑪ 法 定　　fǎdìng
⑫ 节假日　　jiéjiàrì
⑬ 预 约　　yùyuē

文小西：
　　四川博物院真大呀！

大 萌：
　　是的，它大概有一万两千平方米。

江一华：
　　四川博物院里可以看到这么多有意思的东西。
　　我特别喜欢少数民族馆，可以了解到藏族文化、
　　彝族文化和羌族文化。

文小西：
　　我喜欢书画馆，我特别喜欢中国画，尤其是张
　　大千的画。看了这些画，我真想马上去学画画！

大 萌：

太好了！你们在这里都找到了自己喜欢的、想了解
的四川文化。如果你们还想了解更多成都的民俗，
还可以去成都博物馆，就在天府广场附近。

四川博物院在成都市浣花溪历史文化风景区，这是西南
地区最大的综合性博物馆，修建于 1941 年，到现在已经有
70 多年了，四川博物院一共有 14 个展览厅、32 万多件文物。

地址：成都市青羊区浣花南路 251 号
开放时间：每周二至周日
　　　　　（国家法定节假日是周一时不闭馆）
　　　　　夏季 9:00 至 21:00（20:30 停止取票）
　　　　　冬季 9:00 至 20:00（19:30 停止取票）

【二】成都博物馆

（在成都博物馆）

大 萌：

成都博物馆就像一本有关成都的历史书一样，你们
看这个大石头做的"犀牛"，它和都江堰水利工程
有关。你们再看这个小石人，大家猜猜他在做什么。

江 一华：

他在笑，手上有一个鼓，一只脚抬了起来，他一边
跳舞一边打鼓，看上去很有喜感。

① 犀 牛　xīniú
② 鼓　　gǔ
③ 俑　　yǒng
④ 表 演　biǎoyǎn
⑤ 幽 默　yōumò
⑥ 规 模　guīmó
⑦ 木 偶　mù'ǒu
⑧ 皮 影　píyǐng
⑨ 展 示　zhǎnshì
⑩ 讲 座　jiǎngzuò
⑪ 详 细　xiángxì
⑫ 锦城丝管日纷纷，
　半入江风半入云
　jǐnchéngsīguǎnrìfēnfēn,
　bànrùjiāngfēngbànrùyún

大 萌：

没错！这个是"说唱俑"，因为他一边说一边唱，还一边表演，他的表演常常让人们觉得很幽默、很好笑。

文小西：

这个"说唱俑"是汉代的呢，成都很早就有说唱艺术了！

大 萌：

是的，从杜甫的一首诗中就知道成都人是多么热爱音乐啦。

江一华：

我看过这首诗，"锦城丝管日纷纷，半入江风半入云"，对吧？

大 萌：

看来你对杜甫的诗了解不少呢。

江一华：

谢谢夸奖！快来看，这里还有一个陶舞俑。

　　成都博物馆是成都市规模最大的综合型博物馆，已有 50 余年的历史。2016 年 6 月，成都博物馆新馆建成并向游客开放。博物馆有五层，第一层经常有一些特别的展览。二、三、四层展览成都的历史和民俗，五层是中国木偶戏和皮影戏展览。博物馆是新修的，使用了很多高科技展示方法。每年成都博物馆还会举办很多文化讲座和一些特别展览。另外，微信关注成都博物馆，有非常详细的导游讲解和考古人员对某些特别的文物的情况介绍。

地址：青羊区小河街 1 号（天府广场西侧）

开放时间：每周二至周日

（国家法定节假日是周一时不闭馆）

夏季 9:00 至 20:30（19:30 停止取票）

冬季 9:00 至 20:00（19:00 停止取票）

门票价格：免费，可在网上预约

联系电话：028-62915593

【三】金沙遗址博物馆

大 萌：

今天在金沙博物馆，不仅可以逛博物馆，还可以参观现代考古现场。

江 一华：

我第一次看 3000 年以前的文明！那个金面具和"太阳神鸟"太美了。

文 小西：

我喜欢那个介绍 3000 年前成都人民生活的 4D 电影，很精彩。

大 萌：

还有更精彩的呢！我带你们去金沙剧场看音乐剧《金沙》吧，你们一定会更喜欢的。

① 遗址	yízhǐ
② 现场	xiànchǎng
③ 金沙遗址	Jīnshā Yízhǐ
④ 基础	jīchǔ
⑤ 开始	kāishǐ
⑥ 巴蜀	Bāshǔ
⑦ 证据	zhèngjù
⑧ 金器	jīnqì
⑨ 玉	yù
⑩ 悠久	yōujiǔ
⑪ 标志	biāozhì
⑫ 崇拜	chóngbài
⑬ 道	dào
⑭ 光	guāng
⑮ 代表	dàibiǎo
⑯ 季节	jìjié

金沙遗址博物馆在成都的西边，是在金沙遗址的基础上建立的一座遗址博物馆，2007 年开始对游客开放。这个博物馆介绍的是 3000 年前左右（公元前 12 世纪—公元前 7 世纪）的巴蜀文化，可以让我们进一步了解古蜀人民的生活，对蜀文化的研究有非常重要的意义，也为中国古代文明的起源提供了更多的证据。

博物馆里有金器、玉器等各种文物，其中"太阳神鸟"已经成为成都悠久历史的标志。金制的圆形"太阳神鸟"是古成都人对自然的认识，太阳是人们崇拜的神，太阳的 12 道光代表了一年有 12 个月，4 只"神鸟"代表了一年有 4 个季节。在金沙遗址博物馆可以看到遗址的现场，了解文化保护的相关知识。

地址：青羊区金沙遗址路 2 号，青羊大道 227 号

开放时间：夏季 8:00 至 20:00（19:00 停止售票），冬季 8:00 至 18:30（17:30 停止售票）。周一闭馆（1、2、7、8 月及法定节假日除外）

门票价格：80 元 / 人

联系电话：028-87303522

【四】刘氏庄园博物馆

① 氏	shì
② 庄园	zhuāngyuán
③ 地主	dìzhǔ

刘氏庄园博物馆特别有历史意义，它代表着一段重要的历史。刘氏庄园是以前的地主刘文彩的家，代表了四川西部的传统建筑，也代表了过去农村的样子。刘氏庄园也是中国现在保存最好的一个地主的家。

地址：大邑县安仁镇金桂街 15 号

开放时间：9:00—17:00

门票价格：40 元 / 人

联系电话：028-88319959；028-8315113

【五】川菜博物馆

川菜是中国八大菜系之一。来到成都，一定要尝尝地道的川菜，如果还想了解更多川菜的历史，可以去成都西郊的川菜博物馆。那里不仅能了解川菜和川菜文化，还能参观郫县豆瓣的制作过程、学做简单的川菜，如做泡菜、豆浆等。在博物馆里可以免费吃各种成都小吃，免费在茶馆喝茶聊天、打麻将。

地址：郫都区古城镇荣华北巷 8 号

开放时间：9:00—18:00

门票价格：60 元／人

联系电话：028-87918008

①系　　　xì
②郊　　　jiāo
③郫县豆瓣　Píxiàn Dòubàn
④如　　　rú
⑤泡菜　　pàocài
⑥豆浆　　dòujiāng

【六】蜀锦织绣博物馆

①蜀锦织绣　Shǔjǐn Zhīxiù

说到成都，成都的蜀锦和蜀绣也是十分有名的。如果你想了解成都的蜀锦和蜀绣，可以去成都蜀锦织绣博物馆。在那儿不仅能看到各种样式、颜色漂亮的蜀绣蜀锦，还能看到人们是怎么做蜀锦和蜀绣的。

地址：青羊区草堂东路 2 号

开放时间：9:00—17:30

门票价格：免费

联系电话：028-87337990

If you really want to know a city, you can not only go to some streets, eat some snacks, visit some attractions, you also have to go to its museums. In museums we can not only learn more about the history of a city, but also interesting facts. Chengdu is one of the important centers of origin of ancient Chinese civilization and has the largest number of museums nationwide. Entering Chengdu's museums is like entering history, where you converse with historical figures and seemingly go back to the past. The museums not only allow their visitors to gain a deeper understanding of Chengdu's past, but also its present and future.

Part 1 【Sichuan Museum】

Da Meng: Yihua, Xiaoxi, how about going to Sichuan Museum today?

Wen Xiaoxi: All right! Where is the museum? Is it far from here?

Da Meng: Not at all. If we set out now from our school, it'll take us three stops by subway or bus to get there.

(In Sichuan Museum)

Wen Xiaoxi: Sichuan Museum is really big!

Da Meng: It is. It has about 12,000 square meters.

Jiang Yihua: You can see so much interesting stuff inside the museum. I'm particularly fond of the Gallery of Sichuan Ethnic Culture, where you can learn more about Tibetan, Yi and Qiang cultures.

Wen Xiaoxi: I like the Chinese Painting and Calligraphy Gallery. I adore Chinese paintings, especially Zhang Daqian's. Looking at these paintings, I want to learn painting myself right away!

Da Meng: Great! You found here a part of Sichuan culture that you like and want to know more about. If you want to know more Chengdu folk customs, you can also go to Chengdu Museum, which is near Tianfu Square.

Sichuan Provincial Museum is located in Chengdu's Huanhuaxi Historical and Cultural Scenic Area and is the largest comprehensive museum in the southwest of China. It was built in 1941 and thus has existed for more than 70 years now. Sichuan Provincial Museum features a total of 14 exhibition halls and more than 320,000 cultural and historical relics.

Address: No. 251, Huanhua South Road, Qingyang District, Chengdu

Opening Hours: Every Tuesday to Sunday (not closed on Mondays during statutory holidays); summer: 9 am till 9 pm (tickets stop being issued at 8:30 pm); winter: 9 am till 8 pm (tickets stop being issued at 7:30 pm)

Ticket Price: Free, 4,000 tickets are issued every day, online booking available

Tel: 028-65521888 / 65521569

Part 2 【Chengdu Museum 】

(In Chengdu Museum)

Da Meng: Chengdu Museum is like a history book about Chengdu. Look at this rhino made of a big stone, it is connected with the Dujiangyan Water Conservancy Project. Do you see this little stone man? What do you think he is doing?

Jiang Yihua: He's laughing, holding a drum in his hands, raising one foot – he is drumming and dancing and looks very happy.

Da Meng: That's right! That is a "storyteller figurine". Since he talks, sings and also performs, his show is humorous and makes people laugh.

Wen Xiaoxi: This "storyteller figurine" is from the Han Dynasty! The art of talking and singing existed very early in Chengdu!

Da Meng: Yes. Reading Du Fu's poems, you can tell how much Chengdu people love music.

Jiang Yihua: I read this poem! "Zithers and flutes are daily played in town aloud, their sound floats half in river wind and half in cloud", right?

Da Meng: It seems you know a lot about Du Fu's poems.

Jiang Yihua: Thanks for the compliment. Come, they have a dancing earthenware figurine here.

Chengdu Museum is the largest comprehensive museum in Chengdu and has more than 50 years of history. In June 2016, a new gallery was completed and opened to visitors. The museum has five floors: the first floor often shows some special exhibitions. The 2nd, 3rd and 4th floors feature exhibitions from ancient to modern Chengdu in terms of its history and folk customs. The 5th floor exhibits the Chinese puppet show and shadow play. The museum is newly built and uses many high-tech displaying methods. Chengdu Museum holds a lot of cultural lectures and some special exhibitions every year. In addition, if you follow Chengdu Museum on WeChat, you will have access to a very detailed tour guide and brief introductions by archeologists about some special artifacts.

Address: Xiaohe Street, Qingyang District No. 1 (Tianfu Square West Side)

Opening Hours: Every Tuesday to Sunday (not closed on Mondays during statutory holidays); summer: 9 am till 8:30 pm (tickets stop being issued at 7:30 pm); winter: 9 am till 8 pm (tickets stop being issued starting 7:00 pm)

Ticket Price: Free, online booking available

Tel: 028-62915593

Part 3 【Jinsha Site Museum】

Da Meng: Today in Jinsha Site Museum, we can not only look around the museum, and we can also visit a modern archeological site.

Jiang Yihua: This is my first time seeing civilizations from 3,000 years ago! That golden mask and the Golden Sun Bird are stunningly pretty!

Wen Xiaoxi: I like that 4D movie introducing the life of Chengdu people 3,000 years ago. It was fascinating!

Da Meng: And there's even more excitement waiting for us! I'll take you to the "Jinsha Musical" at Jinsha Theater. I'm sure you'll like this one even more.

Jinsha Site Museum is located in the west of Chengdu and established on the basis of the Jinsha Site. It opened to tourists in 2007. The museum introduces the Bashu culture around 3,000 years ago (from the 12th century BC to the 7th century BC), helping visitors gain insight into the life of the people of ancient Shu. The museum is of great significance to the study of Shu culture; it also provides more evidence about the origin of ancient Chinese civilization.

The museum features artifacts such as gold and jade vessels, including the "Golden Sun Bird", which has become a symbol of Chengdu's long history. The ring-shaped, gold-made "Golden Sun Bird" shows the ancient Chengdu people's understanding of the sun, which is their god they would worship. The sun's 12 rays represent the 12 months of the year, the 4 "god birds" represent the 4 seasons. In Jinsha Site Museum, you can see the archaeological site itself and learn more about cultural protection.

Address: No. 2 Jinsha Site Road, No. 227 Qingyang Road, Qingyang District

Opening Hours: Summer: 8 am to 8 pm (ticket sale stops 7 pm); winter: 8 am to 6:30 pm (ticket sale stops 5:30 pm). Closed on Mondays (except January, February, July, August and statutory holidays).

Ticket Price: 80 yuan per person

Tel: 028-87303522

Part 4 【 Liu's Manor Museum 】

Liu's Manor Museum is of particular historic significance, since it represents an important era. Liu's Manor was the home of former landlord Liu Wencai and represents both the traditional architecture of western Sichuan and the appearance of old Chinese villages. Liu's Manor is now also home to China's best landowner.

Address: No. 15 Jingui Street, Anren, Dayi County

Opening Hours: 9 am to 5 pm
Ticket Price: 40 yuan per person
Tel: 028-88319959; 028-8315113

Part 5 【 Sichuan Cuisine Museum 】

The Sichuan cuisine is one of China's eight major cuisines. Visitors to Chengdu must try authentic Sichuan food. If you want to know more about the history of Sichuan cuisine, you can go to the Sichuan Cuisine Museum, located at the western suburbs of Chengdu. There, you can not only gain insight into the Sichuan cuisine and culture, but also watch the Pixian Douban production process, learn to do simple Sichuan dishes, like making pickled vegetables, soy milk and so on. You can eat various Chengdu snacks in the museum for free, and also enjoy free tea in the teahouse while you chat and play mahjong.

Address: No. 8 Ronghua North Alley,GuchengTown, Pidu District

Opening Hours: 9 am to 6 pm

Ticket price: 60 yuan per person

Tel: 028-87918008

Part 6 【 Shu Brocade Embroidery Museum 】

Chengdu's Shu brocade and Shu embroidery are also very famous. If you want to know more, you can go to the Chengdu Shu Brocade Embroidery Museum. There, you can not only see a variety of styles, vibrant Shu brocade and embroidery, but also watch how Shu brocade and embroidery are made.

Address: No. 2 Caotang Road, Qingyang District
Opening Hours: 9 am to 5:30 pm
Ticket Price: Free
Tel: 028-87337990

词语

| 犀牛 | xī niú
rhino | 光 | guāng
ray | 讲座 | jiǎngzuò
lecture |

wén míng 文 明	civilization; culture	qǐ yuán 起 源	origin
rén wù 人 物	figure; personage	wèi lái 未 来	future
shǎo shù 少 数	small number; few; minority	mín zú 民 族	ethnic group
zōng hé 综 合	comprehensive	wén wù 文 物	cultural/ historical relic
tīng 厅	hall	zhǎn guǎn 展 馆	exhibition hall

dì zhǐ 地 址	address
jié jià rì 节 假 日	public holiday
yǒng 俑	figurine
gǔ 鼓	drum
yōu mò 幽 默	humorous
zhǎn shì 展 示	display; show
yí zhǐ 遗 址	site; ruins
jī chǔ 基 础	foundation; base; basis

fǎ dìng 法 定	legal; statutory
yù yuē 预 约	booking; reservation; book
biǎo yǎn 表 演	perform; performance
guī mó 规 模	scale; scope; extent
pí yǐng 皮 影	shadow play
xiàn chǎng 现 场	site, spot
kāi shǐ 开 始	begin; start; commence; initial
zhèng jù 证 据	evidence; proof; testimony

yù 玉	jade
biāo zhì 标 志	sign; mark; symbol
dào 道	measure word for long thin things, e.g. rays
dài biǎo 代 表	represent
shì 氏	family; clan; (after the surname of a famous person)
dì zhǔ 地 主	landlord
jiāo 郊	Suburb
dòu jiāng 豆 浆	soy milk

jīn qì 金 器	gold vessel
yōu jiǔ 悠 久	long; long-standing; age-old (history, tradition, etc.)
chóng bài 崇 拜	worship
guāng 光	light
jì jié 季 节	season
zhuāng yuán 庄 园	manor; mansion; estate
xì 系	system
pào cài 泡 菜	pickled vegetables; pickles

jǐn chéng sī guǎn rì fēn fēn, bàn rù jiāng fēng bàn rù yún
锦 城 丝 管 日 纷 纷, 半 入 江 风 半 入 云

Zithers and flutes are daily played in town aloud; their sound floats half in river wind and half in cloud.

专 有 名 词

1. 藏族   / Zàng zú / Tibetan ethnic group (distributed over the Tibet Autonomous Region, and the provinces of Qinghai, Sichuan, Gansu and Yunnan)

2. 彝族   / Yí zú / Yi ethnic group (distributed over the provinces of Yunnan, Sichuan, Guizhou and the Guangxi Zhuang Autonomous Region)

3. 羌族   / Qiāng zú / Qiang ethnic group (inhabiting Sichuan Province, especially the north)

4. 金沙遗址   / Jīnshā Yízhǐ / Jinsha site

5. 巴蜀   / Bā Shǔ / Bashu

6. 郫县豆瓣   / Píxiàn Dòubàn / Pixian Douban(jiang)

7. 蜀锦织绣   / Shǔjǐn Zhīxiù / Shu brocade and embroidery

语言点

1. 不仅……也……　　2. 如果……话，……
3. 于　　　　　　　　4. 关于
5. 并　　　　　　　　6. 某
7. 不仅……还　　　　8. （比）如……等
9. 说到

思考

1. 你喜欢逛博物馆吗？为什么？
2. 请介绍一下你最喜欢的博物馆。

第五课 Lesson 5

【成都"慢"生活】
【Chengdu's "Slow" Life】

① 享 受　xiǎngshòu
② 方 式　fāngshì
③ 海 洋　hǎiyáng
④ 乐 园　lèyuán
⑤ 滑 冰　huábīng
⑥ 浪 漫　làngmàn
⑦ 高 空　gāokōng
⑧ 旋 转　xuánzhuǎn

　　成都生活，简单地说就是"慢"生活。成都人很会享受舒服、快乐的生活。古人有一句话："少不入蜀，老不离川"，因为四川的生活方式休闲舒服，所以人们认为年轻人最好不要到"蜀"地，老年人不要离开四川。

　　如果你问成都人平时不工作的时候他们常去哪儿玩儿，成都人会告诉你：春熙路、太古里、环球中心或者茶馆。

　　如果说 IFS 和太古里适合年轻时尚的成都人，那么环球中心就适合全家人一起去。因为那儿不仅可以逛商店、看电影、喝咖啡，还可以带孩子去海洋乐园、滑冰，再带家人去看话剧或者画展。想浪漫的话，还可以到 339 高空旋转餐厅欣赏成都的浪漫夜景。

【一】成都的茶馆文化

> **大** 萌：
>
> 　　今天我们去逛逛成都最有名的公园——人民公园。

> **文** 小西：
>
> 　　人民公园里人真多，每个人看起来都很悠闲。

> **大** 萌：
>
> 　　公园里环境好，可以锻炼身体，还可以喝茶、打麻将、聊天。

江一华：
　　来这里喝茶的人这么多啊！

大　萌：
　　是的，"鹤鸣茶馆"——成都最老的茶馆之一，它已经有 90 多年历史了。

文小西：
　　暖暖的太阳，香香的茶，生活真舒服！

江一华：
　　那个人在表演什么功夫呀？

大　萌：
　　那是"功夫茶"。你看他的水壶很有特色！水壶的嘴特别长，他们可以用各种方法帮你加水，像功夫一样，所以就叫"功夫茶"。他们这样的人我们就叫他们"茶博士"。

文小西：
　　我也想试试！

① 功夫　　Gōngfu
② 水壶　　shuǐhú
③ 博士　　bóshì
④ 新式　　xīnshì
⑤ 椅子　　yǐzi
⑥ 生意　　shēngyi
⑦ 戏　　　xì
⑧ 变脸　　biànliǎn
⑨ 滚灯　　gǔndēng

　　想最快地了解成都、了解成都人和成都人的生活，那么一定要去茶馆。成都的茶馆有新式的茶馆，也有比较传统的茶馆。不管是老人还是年轻人，都喜欢到茶馆里来，坐在竹椅子上，泡一杯花茶，跟家人、朋友边喝茶边聊天，或者边喝茶边玩游戏，也可以在茶馆里谈谈生意，写写文章……还可以什么都不做，只是喝茶、坐坐。你还可以选择到川剧院里去，泡一杯茶，欣赏欣赏川剧——变脸、滚灯和皮影戏。

【二】成都的夜生活

大 萌：
　　最近有一首歌特别流行，叫《成都》，你们听过没有？

江一华：
　　当然听过了。上个月老师给我们介绍了这首歌！

大 萌：

那我们去歌里的"小酒馆"坐坐吧。

文 小西：

太好了。在成都晚上出门安全吗？

大 萌：

非常安全，晚上 8 点，成都的"夜生活"才刚开始。晚饭后，老年人喜欢在公园或广场跳舞，锻炼身体。

江 一华：

我经常看到老年人跳舞。那年轻人一般去哪里？

大 萌：

年轻人喜欢约几个朋友去 KTV 唱歌，或者去酒吧听歌、跳舞、喝酒，放松自己。有的人喜欢去路边摊吃烧烤、喝啤酒、摆龙门阵。

文 小西：

看来成都的夜生活很丰富，"小酒馆"在哪里？在玉林路吗？

大 萌：

是的，"小酒馆"在玉林西路。成都的酒吧主要在玉林、九眼桥和兰桂坊。

① 放 松　fàngsōng
② 摆　　　bǎi
③ 龙门阵　lóngménzhèn
④ 丰 富　fēngfù
⑤ 九眼桥　Jiǔyǎn Qiáo
⑥ 兰桂坊　Lánguì Fāng
⑦ 舒 适　shūshì
⑧ 都 市　dūshì

> **文** 小西：
>
> 好，今天我们先去体验一下年轻人的休闲夜生活。走吧，去"小酒馆"。

　　成都人的"夜生活"很丰富，这在全中国都是十分有名的。不管你喜欢热闹、浪漫还是安静、舒适，喜欢传统民俗还是现代都市，成都都能满足你。

Living in Chengdu, simply said, happens at a slow pace. Chengdu people know how to lead a comfortable, happy life. There is an ancient saying, "Sichuan: the young dare not enter; the old dare not leave". Since Sichuan's style of living is one of leisure and comfort, young people are better off not going to Sichuan, while the elderly do not wish to leave.

If you ask somebody from Chengdu, "What do you usually do outside of work? Where do you go to have fun?" They will say, "Chunxi Road, Taikoo Li, the Global Center or the teahouse".

If the IFS and Taikoo Li are suitable for the young and trendy people from Chengdu, then the Global Center is suitable for the whole family, because over there, you can not only stroll around stores, watch movies, or drink coffee, you can also take your children to the marine park, go ice-skating or your entire family to see dramas or art exhibitions. For romantic occasions, you can go to the 339 Revolving Restaurant and enjoy a romantic night in Chengdu.

Part 1 【 Chengdu Teahouse Culture 】

Da Meng: We're going to stroll Chengdu's most famous park today: the People's Park.

Wen Xiaoxi: There are so many people and they all look so relaxed.

Da Meng: The park environment is favorable. You can exercise, drink tea, play mahjong and chat.

Jiang Yihua: There are so many who come here to drink tea!

Da Meng: Yes, because of "Heming Teahouse" – one of Chengdu's oldest teahouses, having existed for more than 90 years.

Wen Xiaoxi: What kind of kung fu is this person over there performing?

Da Meng: That would be "Kung Fu Tea". As you can see, his kettle is very unique! Its mouth is particularly long, which helps them pour water using various methods, which looks just like kung fu, so this tea is called "Kung Fu Tea". We call these people "Tea Master".

Wen Xiaoxi: I also want to have a try!

If you want to get to know Chengdu, Chengdu people and their lives the fastest way, then you must go to a teahouse. Chengdu's teahouses come in modern and traditional styles. The young and the old alike like going to teahouses, have a seat on a bamboo chair, pour a cup of flowering tea, and chat away with family or friends or play some games while enjoying their hot beverage. You can also talk business in the teahouses or do some text production… you can also do nothing at all, just sip some tea and sit. Other than that, you can go to a Sichuan opera, pour a cup of tea and admire Sichuan opera: face-changing, light-rolling and shadow play.

Part 2 【Nightlife in Chengdu】

Da Meng: Lately there has been a particularly popular song called "Chengdu". Have you listened to this song?

Jiang Yihua: Of course we have. Our teacher introduced us to this song!

Da Meng: Then let's go to the "bistro" the lyrics mentioned.

Wen Xiaoxi: Cool! Is it safe to go out in Chengdu at night?

Da Meng: Very safe. Chengdu's nightlife doesn't start until eight in the evening. After dinner, the elderly like to dance in parks or on square to get some exercise.

Jiang Yihua: I often see the elderly dancing. So where do the young people usually go?

Da Meng: Young people like going to KTVs together with friends for karaoke or to bars to listen to some songs, dance, drink and relax. Some like to eat barbecue from street vendors, drink beer and chat.

Wen Xiaoxi: Chengdu's nightlife seems to be varied. Where is the bistro? In Yulin Road?

Da Meng: Yes, the bistro is in Yulin West Road. Chengdu's bars are mainly in Yulin, Jiuyanqiao and Lan Kwai Fong.

Wen Xiaoxi: All right. Today, we're going to try the young people's relaxing nightlife. Let's go to the bistro.

词语

| 乐 | 园 | lèyuán
amusement park |

| 旋 | 转 | xuánzhuǎn
revolve; rotate |

| 水 | 壶 | shuǐhú
kettle |

xiǎng shòu 享 受	enjoy		fāng shì 方 式	style
hǎi yáng 海 洋	ocean		huá bīng 滑 冰	go skating
làng màn 浪 漫	romantic		gāo kōng 高 空	high altitude
gōng fu 功 夫	Kung Fu		bó shì 博 士	doctor; doctorate
xīn shì 新 式	new style; modern		yǐ zi 椅 子	chair

shēng yì 生 意	business
fàng sōng 放 松	relax
lóng mén zhèn 龙 门 阵	chat (Sichuanese)
shū shì 舒 适	comfortable; cosy; snug

xì 戏	drama; play; show
bǎi 摆	place; arrange; (dialect) talk; say
fēng fù 丰 富	rich; abundant; plentiful; varied
dū shì 都 市	big city; metropolis

专 有 名 词

1. 变脸 / Biàn Liǎn/ face-changing

2. 滚灯 / Gǔn Dēng / light-rolling

3. 九眼桥 / Jiǔyǎn Qiáo /Jiuyanqiao (Street); Jiuyan Bridge

4. 兰桂坊 / Lánguì Fāng /Lan Kwai Fong

语言点

1. 如果……那么……   2. 看起来

3. 有特色：有 + 抽象名词   4. 不管

思考

1. 怎样理解"慢"生活？你喜欢"慢"生活还是"快"生活？

2. 请介绍一下在成都你最喜欢的休闲地方。

第六课 【成都的美食】
Lesson 6 【Chengdu Cuisine】

成都又叫"天府之国"，所以成都的食物非常丰富。说到成都美食的味道，人们就会想到麻辣，因为四川人喜欢在做饭时加一些辣椒和花椒。其实成都美食不只是麻辣，也有很多小吃和甜品。当你被成都菜麻得、辣得不得了的时候，来一碗甜甜的冰粉，然后再接着吃麻辣美食。

① 花 椒　　huājiāo
② 其 实　　qíshí
③ 冰 粉　　bīngfěn
④ 烧 烤　　shāokǎo
⑤ 口水鸡　　Kǒushuǐjī
⑥ 龙抄手　　Lóngchāoshǒu
⑦ 红糖糍粑　hóngtáng cíbā

文小西：

　怎么办？我的这件新衣服也不能穿了，又小了。

江一华：

　没办法，你太喜欢吃了，来成都以后你真的吃得有点儿多。

文小西：

　因为成都的美味太多了！火锅、串串、烧烤、冒菜，都是我的最爱！

江一华：

　我喜欢川菜，比如回锅肉、麻婆豆腐、宫保鸡丁，还有成都小吃。

文小西：

　　对对对，担担面、口水鸡、伤心凉粉！

江一华：

　　我比较喜欢龙抄手和钟水饺。

文小西：

　　我是地道的成都"吃货"！我还喜欢成都的冰粉、三大炮、红糖糍粑。

大萌：

　　小西，成都菜那么辣你都能吃，太厉害了。

　　走在成都的大街小巷里，每个地方你都能发现美味的食物，特别是一些很旧、很小的饭馆，味道好，价格便宜，去吃的人也特别多；也有很多有名的美食街，比如一品天下、奎星楼、太古里、小通巷、科华北路……火锅也是成都美食的代表，成都人会把所有的菜都放进火锅里煮着吃。火锅分成都火锅和重庆火锅，成都火锅多使用清油，而重庆火锅多使用牛油，味道更浓厚。

"食在中国，味在四川"，川菜已经走向全世界，成都被联合国教科文组织评为"世界美食之都"。对成都人来说，所有的烦恼、所有的问题都可以用吃来解决。如果你不高兴，成都人会带你去吃好吃的忘掉烦恼；如果你有高兴的事儿，成都人也会带你去吃好吃的庆祝；如果你们要聊工作，成都人会带你一边吃好吃的一边聊；如果你觉得工作太累了，成都人还是会带你去吃东西放松一下……而且还可以每天都带你去吃不一样的美食。

① 旧　　　　jiù
② 一品天下　Yīpǐn Tiānxià
③ 奎星楼　　Kuíxīnglóu
④ 科华北路　Kēhuá Běilù
⑤ 煮　　　　zhǔ
⑥ 清 油　　qīngyóu
⑦ 浓 厚　　nónghòu
⑧ 烦 恼　　fánnǎo
⑨ 解 决　　jiějué

Chengdu, also known as "The Land of Plenty", because Chengdu is rich in food. If you mention the deliciousness of Chengdu's food, people will think about hot and numbing, because the Sichuanese like adding chili and Sichuan peppers to their cooking. In fact, Chengdu cuisine is not only about hot and numbing, it also has many snacks and desserts. When you just cannot bear the Sichuan chili and peppers anymore, have a bowl of sweet bing fen, then continue to eat chilis.

Wen Xiaoxi: What should I do? Another new dress I can't wear! This one, too, got smaller.

Jiang Yihua: There's nothing you can do; you love eating too much. After you've arrived in Chengdu, you've eaten a lot.

Wen Xiaoxi: Because the food here is just so tempting! Hot pot, chuanchuan, barbecue, maocai – I love them all!

Jiang Yihua: I like Sichuan food, like twice-cooked pork, mapo tofu, kung pao chicken as well as Chengdu's snacks.

Wen Xiaoxi: Yes, all of them! Dandan noodles, steamed chicken with chili sauce and sad jelly noodles!

Jiang Yihua: I prefer oil-fried dumplings and Zhong Boiled Dumplings.

Wen Xiaoxi: I'm typical 'Chengdu foodie'! I also like Chengdu's Bingfen, San Da Pao and Hongtang Ciba.

Da Meng: Xiaoxi, Chengdu food is so spicy, but you can still stomach it. You are really amazing.

Walking in the streets of Chengdu, you will find delicious food everywhere, especially in some old, small restaurants, where the food is delicious, the prices low and the patrons many in number. There are also many famous food streets, such as Yipin Tianxia, Kuixing Building, Taikoo Li, Xiao Tong Xiang, Kehua North Road… Hot pot is Chengdu's representative food. The Chengdu people put all their food into hot pot to boil and eat it. Hot pot is divided into Chengdu hot pot and Chongqing hot pot: Chengdu hot pot uses vegetable oil, while Chongqing hot pot uses butter, which makes the taste even stronger.

"Eat in China, savor in Sichuan" – Sichuan has gone global: Chengdu was rated by UNESCO as "Food Capital of the World". For Chengdu people, all troubles and problems can be solved by eating. If you are feeling down, Chengdu people will take you to eat some delicious food to make you forget your troubles. If you are in high spirits, Chengdu people will take you to eat some delicious food in celebration. If you want to talk about work, Chengdu people will talk about work over some good food. If you feel exhausted, Chengdu people will invite you to eat something to let loose…what is more, they will take you to new delicacies every day.

词语

煮	zhǔ
	boil

烦 恼	fánnǎo
	worries

huā jiāo 花 椒	Sichuan pcpper
bīng fěn 冰 粉	bing fen; cold dessert jelly (also comes with toppings, for examples, fermen-ted rice)
shāo kǎo 烧 烤	barbecue
jiù 旧	old
nóng hòu 浓 厚	thick; strong (flavor)

qí shí 其 实	in fact; actually
huǒ guō 火 锅	hot pot
qīng yóu 清 油	(edible) vegetable oil
jiě jué 解 决	solve

专有名词

1. 串串　　　/ chuànchuan / chuan chuan; skewered food

2. 口水鸡　　/ Kǒushuǐjī / steamed chicken with chili sauce; "chicken that makes your mouth water"

3. 龙抄手　　/ Lóngchāoshǒu /long chao shou; oil-fried dumplings

4. 红糖糍粑　/ hóngtáng cíbā / hongtang ciba; brown sugar sticky rice cake

5. 一品天下　/ Yīpǐn tiānxià / Yipin Tianxia

6. 奎星楼　　/ Kuíxīnglóu / Kuixing Building

7. 科华北路　/ Kēhuá Běilù / Kehua North Road

语言点

不得了

思考

1. 你喜欢吃川菜吗？为什么？
2. 请介绍一下你的家乡菜。

第七课 【成都的高新技术园】
Lesson 7 【Chengdu Hi-Tech Industrial Development Zone】

① 公 司　gōngsī
② 实 习　shíxí
③ 感　　gǎn

大 萌:

一华, 听说你在一家公司实习, 是吗?

江一华:

对。这家公司在高新区, 是中国一家有名的软件公司。

文小西:

上个星期一华带我参观了他们公司的展览馆, 给我介绍了他们公司的发展历史, 还给我介绍了他们新做的软件。

大 萌:

挺不错的, 加油, 好好实习。对了, 听说你想搬出宿舍?

江一华:

是的。我想如果我在高新区租一个小公寓, 我每天去公司实习更方便, 而且我也很喜欢高新区的现代感。

文小西:

那你打算毕业后留在成都吗?

④高新区　Gāoxīn Qū
⑤政　府　zhèngfǔ
⑥就　业　jiùyè
⑦创　业　chuàngyè
⑧积　极　jījí
⑨进　步　jìnbù
⑩优　秀　yōuxiù
⑪企　业　qǐyè
⑫人　才　réncái
⑬好　客　hàokè
⑭愉　快　yúkuài
⑮期　待　qīdài

江一华：

　　我没想过这个问题，不过成都这么舒服，高新区的工作机会那么多，而且成都政府对留学生就业也特别支持，能留在这里也是一件好事。

大萌：

　　成都是一个开放的城市，很支持外国人来创业。小西，你做西餐的技术那么好，你可以考虑开一家美味的西餐厅，让更多外国人吃到家乡的味道，让更多成都人吃到美味、地道的西餐。

文小西：

　　好主意，那我可要好好考虑一下。

　　成都——"一座来了就不想离开的城市"。很多人刚开始只是到成都旅行，但是后来就离不开了。

　　成都不仅是一个好看、好玩、好吃的城市，也是"成功之都""机会之城"。几千年来，成都一直是一个积极开放和不断进步的城市。作为中国西南部最重要的城市之一，也为了吸引更多优秀的企业和优秀人才，成都政府给了许多好的机会，越来越多的中国各地和世界各国的人们愿意到成都工作、学习和生活。2013年成都成立了自由贸易试验区，更多的中外企业也在成都开始新的发展。

　　成都风景优美，人们热情好客，相信一定会让你难忘。希望你在成都有一个愉快的旅行，我们也期待与你下次再见！

Da Meng: Yihua, I heard that you're doing an internship, is that true?

Jiang Yihua: Yes. The company is in the Hi-Tech Zone and a well-known software company in China.

Wen Xiaoxi: Yihua took me to the exhibition hall of their company last Monday, where he introduced me to their expansion history and their new software.

Da Meng: Not bad! Give it your all! By the way, I heard that you want to move out of the dormitory?

Jiang Yihua: That's true. I think that it's more convenient to go to work if I rent a small apartment in the Hi-Tech Zone. I also like the modern feel over there.

Wen Xiaoxi: So, do you intend to stay in Chengdu after graduation?

Jiang Yihua: I haven't thought about that yet. Chengdu is so comfortable and there are tons of job opportunities in the Hi-Tech Zone, though. Also, the Chengdu government is especially supportive of overseas students looking for employment. It wouldn't be a bad idea at all to stay here!

Da Meng: Chengdu is a liberal city and very supportive of foreigners starting businesses. Xiaoxi, you're so skilled at cooking western food, so you could consider opening a restaurant serving the best western food, so even more expats may enjoy the taste of their homes and even more Chengdu people can eat delicious, authentic western food.

Wen Xiaoxi: A good idea! I'll have to think about it.

Chengdu: a city you do not want to leave once you have arrived. Many only came to Chengdu for travel, but they saw themselves unable to leave afterwards.

Chengdu is not only a city of pleasantries, fun and food, it is also one of successes and opportunities. For thousands of years, Chengdu has always been a city that has been actively opening up and continuously improving itself. As one of the most important cities in Southwest China, and also to attract more outstanding enterprises and high-skilled workers, the Chengdu government has created many opportunities. More and more people from all parts of China and of other countries in the world are willing to work, study and live in Chengdu. In 2013, a pilot free trade zone was set up in Chengdu, and more Chinese and foreign enterprises start expanding in Chengdu.

Chengdu's scenery is gorgeous, and its people are warm-hearted and hospitable – we are sure your stay will be unforgettable. We hope that you are having a pleasant trip in Chengdu and are looking forward to seeing you next time!

词语

| 人 | 才 | réncái
person of ability; high-skilled worker |

| 好 | 客 | hàokè
hospitable |

| gōng | sī | company, |
| 公 | 司 | firm |

| gǎn | | feel; feeling |
| 感 | | |

| chuàng | yè | start a company |
| 创 | 业 | |

| yōu | xiù | outstanding; |
| 优 | 秀 | excellent |

| qǐ | yè | enterprise; |
| 企 | 业 | business |

| shí | xí | internship |
| 实 | 习 | |

| jiù | yè | looking for employment; getting a job |
| 就 | 业 | |

| jī | jí | active |
| 积 | 极 | |

| jìn | bù | improvement |
| 进 | 步 | |

| rén | cái | person of ability; high-skilled worker |
| 人 | 才 | |

zhèng fǔ 政 府	government
yú kuài 愉 快	delightful, joyful

qī dài 期 待	expect

专 有 名 词

1. 高新区 / Gāoxīng Qū/ Hi-Tech (Industrial Development) Zone

2. 自由贸易试验区 / Zìyóu Màoyì Shìyàn Qū/ pilot free trade zone

语 言 点

1. 好好 +V   2. 越……越……

思 考

1. 学了本书，请说说成都有哪些让你难忘的地方。

2. 你想在中国创业吗？如果创业，你会选择什么样的工作？

参考文献
〔 References 〕

[1] 孔子学院总部 / 国家汉办 . 国际汉语教学通用课程大纲 [M].
北京：北京语言大学出版社，2014.
[2] 马蜂窝 . 成都旅游攻略 [DB/OL].http://www.mafengwo.cn/.
[3] 王宇 . 乐在四川 [M]. 北京：研究出版社，2013.
[4] 三一文化 . 不一样的成都 [M]. 广州：广东旅游出版社，2010.
[5] 飞乐鸟 . 飞乐鸟的手绘旅行笔记：成都 [M]. 北京：人民邮电
出版社，2016.
[6] 成都市委外宣办 .2017 天府成都形象片（英文版）[EB/OL].
http://v.youku.com/v_show/id_XMzAyOTYwNDc4OA====.htm
l?sharefrom=iphone&source=&from=singlemessage&isappinst
alled=0.

图书在版编目（CIP）数据

成都印象/西南财经大学 汉语国际推广成都基地著 —成都：西南财经
大学出版社，2019.7
（走进天府系列教材）
ISBN 987-7-5504-3776-0

Ⅰ.①成… Ⅱ.①西… Ⅲ.①汉语—对外汉语教学—教材②成都—
概况 Ⅳ.①H 195.4②K 927.11
中国版本图书馆 CIP 数据核字（2018）第 241717 号

走进天府系列教材：成都印象·游成都
ZOUJIN TIANFU XILIE JIAOCAI；CHENGDU YINXIANG · YOU CHENGDU
西南财经大学 汉语国际推广成都基地 著

策　　划：王正好　何春梅
责任编辑：李　才
装帧设计：张艳洁
插　　画：辣点设计
责任印制：朱曼丽

出版发行	西南财经大学出版社（四川省成都市光华村街 55 号）
网　　址	http：//www.bookcj.com
电子邮件	bookcj@ foxmail.com
邮政编码	610074
电　　话	028-87353785
照　　排	上海辣点广告设计咨询有限公司
印　　刷	四川新财印务有限公司
成品尺寸	170mm×240mm
印　　张	46.5
字　　数	875 千字
版　　次	2019 年 7 月第 1 版
印　　次	2019 年 7 月第 1 次印刷
印　　数	1—2050 套
书　　号	ISBN 978-7-5504-3776-0
定　　价	198.00 元（套）